Romans Study For Kids

Discovering What It Means To Be Saved

Nicole Love Halbrooks Vaughn

Scripture quotations taken from the *New American Standard Bible*

This book is a product of Proven Path Publications

Proven Path Publications is a part of Proven Path Ministries. A ministry that exists to lead and encourage women. A ministry that strives to help women find the proven path of Christ and to persevere in their journey on it.

All videos are courtesy of *YouTube or Vimeo*

Parental LINKS Advisory: Please check <u>all links</u> before allowing your children to view them. These links could have been altered on the site since the publication of this study.

All images courtesy of *Google Images*

DEDICATION

This Bible study series is dedicated to my two youngest girls, Shelby and Rebekah, who helped me write this as they sat under me as students as I taught through the book of Romans. They were there to let me know if this study helped them understand the truths of this beautiful book of doctrine.

AN OUTLINE OF THE BOOK OF ROMANS

Romans 1:1-17 ------- Introduction
Romans 1:17---------- Theme of the book of Romans

NEED OF SALVATION

Romans 1:18-32------- Sin of the Gentiles
Romans 2-3:8--------- Sin of the Jews
Romans 3:9-20-------- Sin of All

WAY OF SALVATION

Romans 3:21-5-------- Defines Salvation
Romans 3:21-30 (justified by faith apart from Law)
Romans 3:31-4:25 (Abraham is our example of faith)
Romans 5 (our relationship to Adam and Christ)

LIFE OF SALVATION

Romans 6-------------- Dead to Sin
Romans 7------------- Dead to the Law
Romans 8------------- Alive to the Spirit

SCOPE OF SALVATION

Romans 9------------- God's Choice
Romans 10------------ Man's Responsibility
Romans 11------------ Israel Not Forgotten

SERVICE OF SALVATION

Romans 12------------ Present Body as Living Sacrifice
Romans 13------------ Obey Governing Authorities
Romans 14------------ Respect What Matters to Others
Romans 15------------ Accept One Another
Romans 16------------ Goodbye and Final Warnings

CONTENTS

HISTORICAL BACKGROUND

INTRODUCTION

LIFE OF SALVATION

ACKNOWLEDGMENTS

All research on Hebrew translations is from www.biblehub.com

Bible Hub Online Parallel Bible, search and study tools including parallel texts, cross references, Treasury of Scripture, and commentaries. This site provides quick access to topical studies, interlinears, sermons, Strong's and many more resources.

Their mission is best summarized as follows:
1) Increase the visibility and accessibility of the Scriptures online.

2) Provide free access to Bible study tools in many languages.

3) Promote the Gospel of Christ through the learning, study and application of God's word.

This site is a great way to link any verse on your site to an instant menu of 25 versions!

Historical Background for the Book of Romans

Paul was writing to the church in Rome. The church was filled with both Jew and Gentile believers. In this dynamic there arose two groups that were causing dissension and division among the saints in Rome.

The Judaizers taught that one maintained their salvation by keeping the law and rituals of Judaism. They might agree that it was faith in Christ that saved you, but they believed that keeping the law was what kept you saved.

Then there were the Antinomians. This group taught that if you were saved by grace through faith in Jesus then the more you sinned the greater you showed His grace to be.

The Judaizers added to the Word of God and the Antinomians took way.

Paul wrote to the church in Rome to bring the saints together in solid doctrinal truth. He wanted them as well as all the saints everywhere for all time to know the truth that the righteous man shall live by faith. We are saved by faith, kept by faith, and if we are truly saved we will bare the description of being righteous.

INTRODUCTION

This is Part Three of a study through the book of Romans. Part Three in the series will focus on the truths learned in Romans 6 - 8. I wrote this study as I taught a group of Kindergarten through 5th graders. This study is designed to help your children learn how to discover truth for themselves by digging into the Scriptures one verse at a time.

Through this study children can learn how to pay attention to the details. They will learn how to read the Bible while asking who, what, when, where, why, and how. They will learn how Scripture interprets Scripture and how important context is when it comes to understanding the Word of God. To enhance this study simply have your child grab a pen or pencil and some crayons, markers, or colored pencils.

In Part One of our study in the book of Romans we dug deep into *Romans 1 – 3: 20* and learned why we needed to be saved. We learned that Paul was the writer of this letter to the church in Rome. We learned that Paul wanted to help the church work through some issues that were the result of having such diverse backgrounds within the church. Through *Romans 1 – 3:20* we learned that all people, whether they grew up learning the Bible from infancy or whether they had never even heard of the Bible or Jesus, all equally stood as sinners before God.

As we dug into *Romans 3:21 – 5* we discovered the way to be saved was through faith. **Romans 1-5** was written so that we would know why we needed to be saved and who it was that would save us. In **Romans 1-5** we can clearly see that everyone is a sinner. It doesn't matter how good someone thinks they are, they still need Jesus. It doesn't matter how bad someone thinks they are, Jesus still can save them.

Let's do a quick review. I will break down the chapters in Romans that we have studied and you fill in the blanks with what you remember from the chapters. Yes, it's okay to go back and look over the chapters to help you :-)

Romans 1:1-15

_____

_____

_____

_____

Romans 1:16-17 (Remember this is the key verse, so write it out below.)

_____

_____

_____

_____

Romans 1:18-32

_____

_____

_____

_____

Romans 2:1-29

_____

_____

_____

_____

Romans 3:1-18

_____

_____

_____

_____

Romans 3:19-20

_____

_____

_____

_____

Romans 3:21-31

_____

_____

_____

_____

Romans 4:1-25

_____
_____
_____
_____

Romans 5:1-11

_____
_____
_____
_____

Romans 5:12-21

_____
_____
_____
_____

That was a great job reviewing! **Romans 1-5** *explains to us our need for God to save us, because we cannot save ourselves. We also learn in* **Romans 1-5** *that God gave us His Law so that we would realize we needed help. Remember the Law is good. The problem is that we just simply are not. But God loves us anyway! How awesome is that!*

He loves us so much that He sent His Son to die for us... even though we were helpless, ungodly, sinners, who were, at the time, His enemy. We have a very good God!

I think we should thank Him right now. Let's take a moment to pray or sing a song. How about singing "Jesus Loves Me", because He does, and the book of Romans shows us just how much He does.

I'll start. Ready! "Jesus loves me this I know, for the Bible tells me so..."

Now let's grab our pretend shovels and begin digging into Romans 6 - 8. We will begin with Romans 6:1-11.

DIGGING INTO ROMANS 6:1-11

1 What shall we say then? Are we to continue in sin so that grace may increase?

2 May it never be! How shall we who died to sin still live in it?

3 Or do you not know that all of us who have been baptized into Christ Jesus have been baptized into His death?

4 Therefore we have been buried with Him through baptism into death, so that as Christ was raised from the dead through the glory of the Father, so we too might walk in newness of life.

5 For if we have become united with *Him* in the likeness of His death, certainly we shall also be *in the likeness* of His resurrection,

6 knowing this, that our old self was crucified with *Him*, in order that our body of sin might be done away with, so that we would no longer be slaves to sin;

7 for he who has died is freed from sin.

8 Now if we have died with Christ, we believe that we shall also live with Him,

9 knowing that Christ, having been raised from the dead, is never to die again; death no longer is master over Him.

10 For the death that He died, He died to sin once for all; but the life that He lives, He lives to God.

11 Even so consider yourselves to be dead to sin, but alive to God in Christ Jesus.

Romans 6 begins with a question. Read Romans 6:1, what is the question? Circle your answer.

a) are we to have eggs and bacon or pancakes and sausage?

b) are we to use a purple crayon or go with the blue one?

c) are we to continue in sin so that grace may increase?

d) are we to keep on this trail or take another one?

Romans 6:2 answers the question in Romans 6:1. Fill in the blanks with the answer.

May it __ __ __ __ __ __ __!

Look at Romans 6:2 again. Why should we <u>not</u> keep on sinning?

We have __ __ __ __ to sin

Read Romans 6:3. How did we die to sin?

all of us who have been __ __ __ __ __ __ __ __ into Christ Jesus

have been __ __ __ __ __ __ __ __ , into His __ __ __ __ __

Let's look at the word <u>baptized</u> in this verse. This word is "baptizo" in the Greek and it means to dip repeatedly, to immerse, to submerge (of vessels sunk), to cleanse by dipping or submerging, to wash, to make clean with water, to wash one's self, bathe, to overwhelm.

The clearest example that shows the meaning of baptizo is a text from the Greek poet and physician Nicander, who lived about 200 B.C. It is a recipe for making pickles and is helpful because it uses both words.

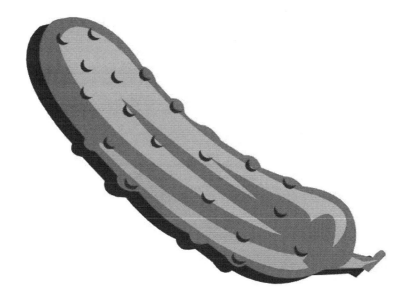

Nicander says that in order to make a pickle, the vegetable should first be 'dipped' or baptized (bapto) into boiling water and then 'baptized' (baptizo) in the vinegar solution. Both verbs concern the immersing of vegetables in a solution. But the first is temporary. The second, the act of baptizing the vegetable, produces a permanent change.

The word "baptized" in **Romans 6** *is the one that makes the cucumber into a pickle.*

Now, can that pickle ever become a cucumber again? Circle your answer.

Yes   No

Read Romans 6:4-6. Next is a storyboard. Draw out what each verse says happened to you if you were baptized into Christ.

Read Romans 6:7. If we have died what are we free from?

— — —

What was our relationship to sin before we died with Jesus (was baptized into Christ)? Read Romans 6:6 to find the answer.

We were __ __ __ __ __ __ to sin

Does a slave have any control over his or her own life?

Yes   No

If we have died with Christ and are now freed from sin, does that mean that we now have control over our own life?

Yes   No

Can sin still tell us what to do and make us do it?

Yes   No

Does sin ever try to make us its slave again?

Yes   No

Read Romans 6:8. If we have died with Christ what will we also do with Him?

__ __ __ __

Read Romans 6:9. What do we know now that Christ has risen from the dead? Will He ever die again?

Yes   No

How can we know He will never die again? What is no longer master over Him? Unscramble the letters to find your answer.

HEDAT   __ __ __ __ __

Read Romans 6:10. How many times did Jesus have to die to sin? Circle your answer.

Several   Couple   Once   Over and Over

How does Jesus live the life that He lives?

to   __ __ __

Read Romans 6:11. How does this verse begin? Fill in the blanks.

E __ v __   s __

This phrase in the Greek is kai houto and it means and also in this manner.

Read Romans 6:11 again. What are we to consider ourselves to be? Draw a picture of yourself under the correct answer.

alive to sin, but dead to God	dead to sin, but alive to God

*The word "consider" in **Romans 6:11** is in present tense and is in a command form, so it means to "keep on considering". God wants us to remember <u>every day</u> that we are to be dead to sin and alive to Him in Jesus. How about writing **Romans 6:11** on a card, and put it on your bathroom mirror and read it every morning for at least this next week :-)*

****

DIGGING INTO ROMANS 6:12-23

12 Therefore do not let sin reign in your mortal body so that you obey its lusts,

13 and do not go on presenting the members of your body to sin *as* instruments of unrighteousness; but present yourselves to God as those alive from the dead, and your members *as* instruments of righteousness to God.

14 For sin shall not be master over you, for you are not under law but under grace.

15 What then? Shall we sin because we are not under law but under grace? May it never be!

16 Do you not know that when you present yourselves to someone *as* slaves for obedience, you are slaves of the one whom you obey, either of sin resulting in death, or of obedience resulting in righteousness?

17 But thanks be to God that though you were slaves of sin, you became obedient from the heart to that form of teaching to which you were committed,

18 and having been freed from sin, you became slaves of righteousness.

19 I am speaking in human terms because of the weakness of your flesh. For just as you presented your members as slaves to impurity and to lawlessness, resulting in *further* lawlessness, so now present your members as slaves to righteousness, resulting in sanctification.

20 For when you were slaves of sin, you were free in regard to righteousness.

21 Therefore what benefit were you then deriving from the things of which you are now ashamed? For the outcome of those things is death.

22 But now having been freed from sin and enslaved to God, you derive your benefit, resulting in sanctification, and the outcome, eternal life.

23 For the wages of sin is death, but the free gift of God is eternal life in Christ Jesus our Lord.

*We learned in **Romans 6:1-11** that when we are saved by grace through faith we are baptized into Jesus Christ, which means that...*

- when He died, we died

- when He was buried, we were buried

- when He was raised, we were raised

- death is no longer master over Him

- sin is no longer master over us

- and since Jesus lives to God, so should we

*Now we are going to begin digging into **Romans 6:12-23**...*

Read Romans 6:12. What word does it begin with?

— — — — — — — — — —

*Remember that when we see a "therefore" we need to look back at the verses before it to see what the "therefore" is there for. Read **Romans 6:8-11** to find out what the "therefore" is there for.*

Read Romans 6:12 again. What command does God give us in this verse?

Do not let __ __ __ reign in your mortal __ __ __ __

Read Romans 6:13. What command are we given in this verse?

Do not go on presenting the members of your body to

__ __ __ as instruments of unrighteousness

Read Romans 6:13 again. Who and what are we to present ourselves to?

to __ __ __ as those alive from the dead, and your members as instruments of

__ __ __ __ __ __ __ __ __ __ __ __ __ to God

Read Romans 6:14. How are we able to present our body to God as an instrument of righteousness?

For __ __ __ shall __ __ __ be master over you

Read Romans 6:14 again. As a Christian, sin is no longer master over you and death is no longer master over you. So according to this verse what are we under? Circle your answer.

law   grace

Read Romans 6:15. If we are under grace and not law, does that mean that we can sin whenever we want to?

May it __ __ __ __ __ be!

Read Romans 6:16-22. Now that we are freed from sin, does that mean that we are slaves to no one and nothing?

Read through these verses and answer the questions below.

If you have been freed from sin, <u>what</u> are you now a slave to? (*Hint: look at Romans 6:18*)

__ __ __ __ __ __ __ __ __ __ __ __

If you have been freed from sin, <u>Who</u> are you now enslaved to? (*Hint: look at Romans 6:22*)

__ __ __

When you were a slave to sin, you obeyed sin. What does the Bible tell us is the result of obeying sin? Read Romans 16:16 to find the answer.

— — — — —

When you become a slave to God, you obey righteousness. What does the Bible tell us is the result of obeying righteousness? Read Romans 16:19 to find the answer.

— — — — — — — — — — — — — —

When we become a Christian we get a new heart and a new master. This changes the way we live and the choices we make. Have you ever seen "The Grinch Who Stole Christmas"?

Type this link into your computer search bar: http://www.youtube.com/watch?v=_eulSbXIjzk and watch the video clip.

Or if you have the movie at home, why not watch it with your family.

THINK ABOUT IT...

How did the Grinch change when his heart changed? Did his actions change? Did he get strength to do the right thing?

****

Romans 16:16-22 explains to us the difference in obeying sin and obeying righteousness. When we obey righteousness we learn the result is our sanctification.

Sanctification is a big word! It is a big and important word. As a matter of fact it is what Romans 6 - 8 is all about. So what exactly is sanctification?

Sanctification is the purification of our heart and life. Justification is when God forgives us and declares us not guilty of sin because Jesus paid our debt for us. Sanctification is when God begins to make us look and act like His children.

Read Romans 16:22 again. What is the outcome of sanctification?

— — — — — — — — — — —

Read Romans 16:23. Right this verse out below. This one you need to memorize.

_____

_____

_____

THINK ABOUT IT...

Did you first begin the process of sanctification (making yourself pure) by obeying righteousness (keeping the law) and then earn your justification (pardon from sin) from God and receive eternal life?

Is it even possible for us to do that?

No it's not.

That's why eternal life is a gift from God.

*Remember Jesus is a gift to us from God (**John 3:16**). Justification is a gift to us from God in Jesus (**Romans 3:24**). Righteousness is a gift to us from God through Jesus (**Romans 4:3**). Sanctification is a result of the gifts of God to Jesus (**Romans 6:22**).*

We can't make ourselves good enough for God. God has to do that for us.

How about we take a moment to tell God "thank You!"

****

15

DIGGING INTO ROMANS 7:1-6

Wow! The truth you learned in Romans 6 is life changing! Do you know that there are grown ups, who have been going to church for years and years who do not know what you just learned. Let's keep going as we dig into Romans 7.

Romans 7:1-6

1 Or do you not know, brethren (for I am speaking to those who know the law), that the law has jurisdiction over a person as long as he lives?

2 For the married woman is bound by law to her husband while he is living; but if her husband dies, she is released from the law concerning the husband.

3 So then, if while her husband is living she is joined to another man, she shall be called an adulteress; but if her husband dies, she is free from the law, so that she is not an adulteress though she is joined to another man.

4 Therefore, my brethren, you also were made to die to the Law through the body of Christ, so that you might be joined to another, to Him who was raised from the dead, in order that we might bear fruit for God.

5 For while we were in the flesh, the sinful passions, which were *aroused* by the Law, were at work in the members of our body to bear fruit for death.

6 But now we have been released from the Law, having died to that by which we were bound, so that we serve in newness of the Spirit and not in oldness of the letter.

Read Romans 7:1. How does it begin?

__ __ do you not know,

THINK ABOUT IT...

*How many complete thought sentences do you know that begin with the word "or"? "Or" is a conjunction word. This means it joins together two sentences, or two thoughts by comparing, contrasting, or conjoining them. If **Romans 7** begins with the word "or" then we need to find out what two sentences or thoughts are being joined together. So let's go back and begin reading at **Romans 6:20.***

Read Romans 6:20-7:1. How long does the law have jurisdiction over a person?

__ __ __ __ __ __ __ __ __ __ __ __ __ __ __ __ __

Read Romans 7:2-3. What example does Paul give us to explain how the law was over us? Unscramble the words to get your answer.

MIRAREGA   __ __ __ __ __ __ __ __

THINK ABOUT IT...

Have you ever been to a wedding? When the couple getting married says their wedding vows, or wedding promises to one another, that promise ends with "until death do us part"

The husband and wife are supposed to keep these promises to one another and make them with no one else. These promises to one another are for life.

But if one of them dies, then the promises can be made to someone else.

*Paul is trying to show us here that we are bound to the law until we die in Christ like we learned happens **Romans 6**.*

It's kind of like we are married to the law. But when we die in Christ, the law does not matter anymore, because we are now free to be married to Jesus.

Read Romans 7:4. What usually happens when people get married? Look at the picture below to get your answer.

They have __ __ __ __ __ __

Read Romans 7:4 again. If we have died to the law and have been married to Christ what should we be doing for God?

__ __ __ __ __ __ __   __ __ __ __ __

Remember what we learned in our Romans Part One Study? Go back and read Matthew 7:16-20 and John 15:1-8. Then answer the question below.

How do we know if we belong to God?

We should bear __ __ __ __ fruit for __ __ __

Read Romans 7:5. When we were in the flesh what did our bodies bear fruit for?

__ __ __ __ __

Read Romans 7:6. When we were bound to the Law we served in the oldness of the letter. No matter how hard we tried to keep the Law, we just couldn't. Now in Jesus we are dead to the Law. How do we serve now?

in the __ __ __ __ __ __ of the __ __ __ __ __

Read Galatians 5:22-23. This passage describes to us what our fruit should be when we serve in the Spirit. Fill the tree below with the fruit of the Spirit.

****

7 What shall we say then? Is the Law sin? May it never be! On the contrary, I would not have come to know sin except through the Law; for I would not have known about coveting if the Law had not said, "You shall not covet."

8 But sin, taking opportunity through the commandment, produced in me coveting of every kind; for apart from the Law sin *is* dead.

9 I was once alive apart from the Law; but when the commandment came, sin became alive and I died;

10 and this commandment, which was to result in life, proved to result in death for me;

11 for sin, taking an opportunity through the commandment, deceived me and through it killed me.

12 So then, the Law is holy, and the commandment is holy and righteous and good.

13 Therefore did that which is good become *a cause of* death for me? May it never be! Rather it was sin, in order that it might be shown to be sin by effecting my death through that which is good, so that through the commandment sin would become utterly sinful.

Romans 7:7 begins with more questions. What are they?

a)   What shall we say then?

b)   _ _ _   the _ _ _ _   _ _ _ _?

Read Romans 7:7 again. What is Paul's answer to these questions?

_ _ _   _ _   _ _ _ _ _ _   _ _!

What does Paul say that he would not have come to know had it not been for the Law?

— — —

THINK ABOUT IT...

How does knowing the Ten Commandments help you know when you are sinning? When you tell a lie, take something that is not yours, disobey your parents, or even want something that belongs to someone else... do the Ten Commandments and other verses you have learned from the Bible remind you of what God says about sin?

Read Romans 7:8-11. This might be hard to understand as you read it, so go ahead and read it two times.

*Now maybe **what Romans 7:8-11** is saying is that, before you knew God's Law, you probably thought you were pretty good. When you heard God's Law the first time, you might even have thought you could do a pretty good job of keeping it.*

Look up and read Matthew 19:16-22. You will read about a man who thought he could keep all the commandments too.

According to Matthew 19:21 what did Jesus say that the young man still needed to do?

_ _ _ _ _ all his _ _ _ _ _ _ _ _ _ _ _ _ _

and come, _ _ _ _ _ _ _ _ _ _

What commandment or commandments do you think the young man was unable to keep? Write your answer below.

_____

_____

_____

THINK ABOUT IT...

As you read Romans 7:7-11 and you read about the young man in Matthew 19:16-22 do you think that the Law is bad since it was because of the Law that sin was woken up in you?

Go back and read Romans 1:18-20, Romans 2:12-16, and Romans 3:19-20.

What did these verses teach us about the Law of God?

So is the Law good or is the Law bad? Explain your answer to the adult that is helping you with this study.

Read Romans 7:12. What does this verse tell us about the Law of God? Fill in the blanks below with the answer.

the Law is __ __ __ __

the commandment is __ __ __ __

    and __ __ __ __ __ __ __ __

    and __ __ __ __

Read Romans 7:13. How does this verse begin? Unscramble the letters to get your answer.

HTREEFROE   __ __ __ __ __ __ __ __ __

Remember when there is a "therefore" we need to find out what the "therefore" is there for. This "therefore" is referring back to what we just learned, that the Law is good.

Read Romans 7:13 again.

What is Paul's question?

did that which is good become a cause of __ __ __ __ __ for __ __?

What is the answer to this question?

__ __ __   __ __   __ __ __ __ __ __   __ __!

Read Romans 7:13 again. What is it that causes death in us. Circle your answer.

Law   sin

Read Romans 7:13 one more time. What good thing does the Law do for us?

it makes sin __ __ __ __ __ __ __   __ __ __ __ __ __ __

Whew! That was a lot! We will stop here and think about all that we have learned. Let's end today's study with talking to our God. Let's thank Him that we are saved by faith in Jesus and not our ability to keep the Law.

****

14 For we know that the Law is spiritual, but I am of flesh, sold into bondage to sin.

15 For what I am doing, I do not understand; for I am not practicing what I *would* like to *do*, but I am doing the very thing I hate.

16 But if I do the very thing I do not want *to do*, I agree with the Law, *confessing* that the Law is good.

17 So now, no longer am I the one doing it, but sin which dwells in me.

18 For I know that nothing good dwells in me, that is, in my flesh; for the willing is present in me, but the doing of the good *is* not.

19 For the good that I want, I do not do, but I practice the very evil that I do not want.

20 But if I am doing the very thing I do not want, I am no longer the one doing it, but sin which dwells in me.

21 I find then the principle that evil is present in me, the one who wants to do good.

22 For I joyfully concur with the law of God in the inner man,

23 but I see a different law in the members of my body, waging war against the law of my mind and making me a prisoner of the law of sin which is in my members.

24 Wretched man that I am! Who will set me free from the body of this death?

25 Thanks be to God through Jesus Christ our Lord! So then, on the one hand I myself with my mind am serving the law of God, but on the other, with my flesh the law of sin.

Yesterday we learned that the Law of God is good, righteous, and holy. We learned that the Law helps us see how very sinful our sin really is. Without the Law we would convince ourselves that our sin was really not that bad. Especially when we compared our sin to others. We can always find someone whose sin we think is worse than ours.

However, what we learn from the Bible is that all of us are equally judged by the Law of God and none of us can keep it. That is why we need Jesus.

*Today we are picking up our study in Romans in **Romans 7:14-25**. Today we will see that even after we are saved we are still at war with sin.*

*That's why God gave us armor. Before we study today take a moment to go read **Ephesians 6:10-18**. Let's put our armor on and pray that God would help us understand His Word and help us obey it*

*Now let us begin today's study with reading **Romans 7:14-25**.*

Read Romans 7:14.

What do we learn about the Law?

It is __ __ __ __ __ __ __ __ __ __

What do we learn about ourselves?

I am of __ __ __ __ __, sold into __ __ __ __ __ __ __ to __ __ __

Read Romans 7:15 very slowly. Fill in the blanks below to complete the verse.

For what I am doing,

__ __ __ __ __ __ __ __ __ __ __ __ __ __ __ __ __ __

for I am not practicing what I would like to do, but

__ __ __ __ __ __ __ __ the very thing I __ __ __ __

THINK ABOUT IT...

Have you ever felt like Paul in Romans 7:15? Have you ever wanted to do the right thing, because you knew it was right, but instead you did something that knew was wrong? Maybe you told your mom or dad or brother or sister or even your best friend that you hated them, when you know you don't, but when your feeling were hurt or you were angry it just came out. Then you felt really bad for saying it... and feeling it.

Read <u>Romans 7:16</u>. What does it show about us, when we know that something we did was wrong and we really hate that we did it?

it shows we __ __ __ __ __ with the __ __ __ ,

confessing that the __ __ __ is __ __ __ __

*Now if we confess that the Law is good and the problem is us, not the Law of God. And, if we have confessed Jesus as Lord and we have been united with Him in His death, burial, and resurrection (remember **Romans 6:3-4**). Why do we still sin?*

Let's read Romans 7:17-19 very slowly to find out. Fill in the blanks below to complete the verses as you read.

So now, no longer am __ the __ __ __ doing __ __, but __ __ __ which __ __ __ __ __ __ in __ __

For I know that __ __ __ __ __ __ __ __ __ __ __ dwells in __ __, that is __ __ __ __ __ __ __ __

for the __ __ __ __ __ __ __ is present in __ __, but the __ __ __ __ __ __ of the __ __ __ __ is __ __ __

For the __ __ __ __ __ that I __ __ __ __ , I do __ __ __ do, but I __ __ __ __ __ __ __ __ the very __ __ __ __ __ that I __ __ __ __ __ want

Read Romans 7:20. What is the cause of all this struggle inside of us?

the __ __ __ which __ __ __ __ __ __ in me

THINK ABOUT IT...

Do you know any Christians who got a new body after they were saved? No? Me either. I still have my old one too. When we become Christians and Jesus comes to live in us, our sin is still in us too. The difference is that now that sin is no longer our boss. Jesus is. So now we have Jesus to help us fight sin and to help us not sin. When before we were Christians, we had no power over sin. We may not even have recognized that some things were a sin. So now as Christian, we have a struggle with this flesh of ours that still wants to do bad things sometimes, and our hearts that want us to do the good and right things that please God.

Go to a computer and put this link in your search bar, it's a video from Candace that kind of helps you see this struggle in action.

http://www.youtube.com/watch?v=9iq6Cbd5YxA

Read Romans 7:21. What does this struggle reveal to us?

1) __ __ __ __ is present in me

2) but I want to __ __   __ __ __ __

Read Romans 7:22. Where do we joyfully concur (or agree) with the law of God?

in the __ __ __ __ __   __ __ __

Read Romans 7:23. Where do we see the different law (the law of sin)?

in the members of my __ __ __ __

Read Romans 7:23 again. What is happening between the different law at work in the members of our body and the law of our mind that knows God's law is good?

they are at __ __ __

THINK ABOUT IT...

Do you think that even as a Christian you could go a whole week and never sin?

Read Romans 7:24. What conclusion do we come to when we try not to sin and to keep the Law of God?

__ __ __ __ __ __ __ __ man that I am!

Do you know what "wretched" means? It means poor, miserable, despicable, and absolutely pitiful! The harder we try to keep God's law on our own, the more we realize we can't.

Read Romans 7:24 again. What question is asked?

__ __ __ will set me __ __ __ __ from the body of this __ __ __ __ __?

Read Romans 7:25. Who is the "Who" that will set us free?

__ __ __ __ __

WOW! Jesus saves us today from the power of sin and the effects of sin, and one day He will save us from this body of sin as well. We will learn more about this in Romans 8. Right now let's just stop here for the day and spend some time thanking God for Jesus. Why not sing the first part of Amazing Grace as a praise to God right now.

******

DIGGING INTO ROMANS 8:1-8

1 Therefore there is now no condemnation for those who are in Christ Jesus.

2 For the law of the Spirit of life in Christ Jesus has set you free from the law of sin and of death.

3 For what the Law could not do, weak as it was through the flesh, God *did*: sending His own Son in the likeness of sinful flesh and *as an offering* for sin, He condemned sin in the flesh,

4 so that the requirement of the Law might be fulfilled in us, who do not walk according to the flesh but according to the Spirit.

5 For those who are according to the flesh set their minds on the things of the flesh, but those who are according to the Spirit, the things of the Spirit.

6 For the mind set on the flesh is death, but the mind set on the Spirit is life and peace,

7 because the mind set on the flesh is hostile toward God; for it does not subject itself to the law of God, for it is not even able *to do so*,

8 and those who are in the flesh cannot please God.

Today begin reading at Romans 7:21 and read through Romans 8:1.

What does Romans 7:25 say that we serve with our mind?

the __ __ __ of __ __ __

What does Romans 7:25 say that we serve with our flesh?

the __ __ __ of __ __ __

THINK ABOUT IT...

Have you ever played a game of tug-o-war? I bet you have. Have you ever played a game of tug-of-war when you were the one in the middle?

Maybe you have had two friends before who did not get along with each other, but you wanted to be friends with both of them. How did that make you feel?

Maybe those friends did not get along because one of them wanted you to do things that you knew were wrong and the other friend simply would not do it... but you were torn between the two friends.

*This type of struggle and tug-of-war is what goes on inside of us as Christians, but **Romans 8:1** is our hope!*

Read Romans 8:1 again and this time read it out loud.
Below is a picture outline of Jesus. Where does Romans 8:1 say that you are? (Hint: find the preposition)

What does Romans 8:1 tell us about those who are in Christ Jesus?

now __ __   __ __ __ __ __ __ __ __ __ __ __ __ __ __

Condemnation is to judge and punish. Do you remember what the wages of sin is? (Hint: read Romans 6:23)

__ __ __ __ __

Who took your punishment and judgment?

__ __ __ __ __

Can you look back through Romans and write down the address of the verses that tell us that Jesus died for your sin?

_____

_____

_____

Read Romans 8:2. What has set you free from the law of sin and of death?

the law of the __ __ __ __ __ __ of __ __ __ __

What is the law of the Spirit? Go back and read Romans 1:16. What is the power of salvation?

the __ __ __ __ __ __

The Gospel is the power of salvation because it is also the law of the Spirit. The law of the Spirit works with the Law of God to set you free from the law of sin and death!

Read Romans 8:3. Why was the Law of God not enough by itself?

because of our __ __ __ __ __

NICOLE LOVE HALBROOKS VAUGHN

Read Romans 8:3 again. What did God do for us since He knew we were unable to keep the Law of God because of our flesh?

He sent __ __ __   __ __ __ in the likeness of sinful __ __ __ __ __ and as an offering for sin

Take a moment to say John 3:16. Does this verse help you understand what Romans 8:3 says God did for us? Circle your answer.

Yes   No   I don't know

Read Romans 8:3 one more time. What does it say that Jesus did for us when He came in the flesh?

He __ __ __ __ __ __ __ __ __ __ sin in the flesh.

Read Romans 8:4. Why did Jesus need to condemn sin in the flesh?

so that the __ __ __ __ __ __ __ __ __ __ __ __ __ of the __ __ __ might be

__ __ __ __ __ __ __ __ __ in us

THINK ABOUT IT...

Sin came to punish and judge us... but Jesus came and punished and judged sin. This word for "condemned" tells us that when we are baptized in Jesus, when we believe in Him, when we died with Him, were buried with Him, and were raised with Him... He took away sins power and dominion over us. In Jesus, sin is no longer our boss. Sin can no longer condemn us. Even if it tries to kill us. Jesus will raise us from the dead because He is our boss now.

Think about the preposition "in". When you are "in" something it gives you your position, your place.

Romans 8:1 begins to teach us that the reason we are now from sin's power and judgment is because of who we are IN, and now we will begin to see that we are now becoming able to obey God and His laws because of who we are in and because of who is IN us.

The word "but" is important in the Bible and so is the word "in". They are little words with BIG meaning. When you read through the verses in the Bible it is a smart thing to pay close attention to all the buts, ins, withs, ifs, ors and ands. They will teach you a lot about God and your relationship with Him.

Read Romans 8:4 again. How do those who are in Christ walk? Circle your answer.

according to the flesh   according to the Spirit

Read Romans 8:5-7. There is a comparison between two minds. A mind set of the flesh and a mind set on the Spirit. Draw a line to the correct descriptions.

MIND SET ON THE FLESH   death

                                                   life

MIND SET ON THE SPIRIT   peace

                                                   hostile toward God

                                                   doesn't subject to law of God

                                                   not able to subject to law of God

Read Romans 8:8. Can those who are in the flesh please God? Circle your answer.

Yes   No

Does what you learned in Romans 8:5-7 help you understand why those in the flesh cannot please God? Circle your answer.

Yes   No

****

DIGGING INTO ROMANS 8:9-17

9 However, you are not in the flesh but in the Spirit, if indeed the Spirit of God dwells in you. But if anyone does not have the Spirit of Christ, he does not belong to Him.

10 If Christ is in you, though the body is dead because of sin, yet the spirit is alive because of righteousness.

11 But if the Spirit of Him who raised Jesus from the dead dwells in you, He who raised Christ Jesus from the dead will also give life to your mortal bodies through His Spirit who dwells in you.

12 So then, brethren, we are under obligation, not to the flesh, to live according to the flesh—

13 for if you are living according to the flesh, you must die; but if by the Spirit you are putting to death the deeds of the body, you will live.

14 For all who are being led by the Spirit of God, these are sons of God.

15 For you have not received a spirit of slavery leading to fear again, but you have received a spirit of adoption as sons by which we cry out, "Abba! Father!"

16 The Spirit Himself testifies with our spirit that we are children of God,

17 and if children, heirs also, heirs of God and fellow heirs with Christ, if indeed we suffer with *Him* so that we may also be glorified with *Him*.

Read Romans 8:9 very carefully. This is a very important verse. We find several of our <u>very important words</u> in this verse. The verse is printed below. Read it and circle the words: *but, in, if*

However, you are not in the flesh but in the Spirit, if indeed the Spirit of God dwells in you. But if anyone does not have the Spirit of Christ, he does not belong to Him.

According to the word <u>but</u>, is the subject (the you) of this verse in the flesh or in the Spirit? Circle your answer.

in the flesh   in the Spirit

According to what you learned from circling the word *if,* what allows a person <u>to not</u> be in the flesh? What or Who must they have?

the __ __ __ __ __ __ of __ __ __

According to what you learned from circling the word *in,* where does the Spirit of God need to be for you to belong to God?

__ __   __ __ __

If the Spirit of God, the Spirit of Christ, is in you then you belong to God. Read Romans 8:10. Who else is in you if you belong to God?

__ __ __ __ __ __

Read Romans 8:10 again. Fill in the blanks below. Then answer the questions.

the __ __ __ __ is __ __ __ __ because of __ __ __

the __ __ __ __ __ __ is __ __ __ __ __ because of __ __ __ __ __ __ __ __ __ __ __ __ __ __

If Christ is in you what is dead and why?

_____

If Christ is in you what is alive and why?

_____

Read Romans 8:11. If the Spirit of Christ dwells in us what will God one day also give life to?

our __ __ __ __ __ __

THINK ABOUT IT...

*Go back and read **Romans 6:3-6** and **Romans 7:21-25** and remember what you learned from these passages to help you understand **Romans 8:9-11**.*

*Now look at **Romans 8:9-11** again. How many times did you read the words "dwells in you".*

Take a moment right now to ask God if His Spirit dwells in you.

Read Romans 8:12-13. If the Spirit of God and Jesus are in us, who are we obligated to listen to? Circle your answer.

our flesh/body   the Spirit of God

Read Romans 8:14. Who must lead you for you to belong to God as His son or daughter?

the __ __ __ __ __ __ of __ __ __

Read Romans 8:15. What kind of spirit do you no longer have if you belong to God?

a spirit of __ __ __ __ __ __ __ __

According to Romans 8:15, where did this spirit of slavery lead you?

to __ __ __ __

According to Romans 8:15, if you belong to God what kind of spirit do you now have?

a spirit of __ __ __ __ __ __ __ __

What does this spirit of adoption allow us to call God?

Abba! __ __ __ __ __ __!

Read Romans 8:16. Who testifies with our spirit to let us know that we are children of God?

the __ __ __ __ __ Himself

THINK ABOUT IT...

Do you know what "testifies" means?

Have you ever been playing at the park and saw your mom or dad talking to someone you did not know? Then, they called you out from all the other kids and introduced you to the person they were talking to and your mom or dad said, "This one is mine."

*Well, that is kind of like what the word "testifies" in **Romans 8:16** means.*

Read Romans 8:17. If you are a child of God what are you also?

__ __ __ __ __ also, __ __ __ __ __ __ of God and fellow __ __ __ __ __ with Christ

NICOLE LOVE HALBROOKS VAUGHN

THINK ABOUT IT...

An heir is someone who is entitled by law to receive the things of another person, their house, land, and belongings. It also is a person who would be next in line to receive a certain position of authority.

Let's do some cross-referencing, which means let's look at some other Scriptures to help us see what we are heir to if we are children of God.

*Take a moment to look up and read **John 14:1-3** and **Revelation 21:1-7.***

Read Romans 8:17 again. Find the word "if". What must we do in order to be a child of God and be an heir with Christ?

if indeed we __ __ __ __ __ __ with Him

THINK ABOUT IT...

What does it mean to suffer with Him? How do we suffer with Jesus? Just think about it. We will study more later.

****

18 For I consider that the sufferings of this present time are not worthy to be compared with the glory that is to be revealed to us.

19 For the anxious longing of the creation waits eagerly for the revealing of the sons of God.

20 For the creation was subjected to futility, not willingly, but because of Him who subjected it, in hope

21 that the creation itself also will be set free from its slavery to corruption into the freedom of the glory of the children of God.

22 For we know that the whole creation groans and suffers the pains of childbirth together until now.

23 And not only this, but also we ourselves, having the first fruits of the Spirit, even we ourselves groan within ourselves, waiting eagerly for *our* adoption as sons, the redemption of our body.

24 For in hope we have been saved, but hope that is seen is not hope; for who hopes for what he *already* sees?

25 But if we hope for what we do not see, with perseverance we wait eagerly for it.

26 In the same way the Spirit also helps our weakness; for we do not know how to pray as we should, but the Spirit Himself intercedes for *us* with groanings too deep for words;

27 and He who searches the hearts knows what the mind of the Spirit is, because He intercedes for the saints according to *the will of* God.

*Have you considered what it means for you to suffer with Jesus? Well let's begin to think about this by looking at **Romans 8:18**.*

Read Romans 8:18. What does Paul tell us about the sufferings of this present time? Are they worthy to be compared with the glory that is to be revealed to us? Circle your answer.

Yes   No

Read Romans 8:19. What does creation wait eagerly for?

the __ __ __ __ __ __ __ __ __ of the sons of __ __ __

Read Romans 8:20-21. What do you learn about the creation?

it was subjected to __ __ __ __ __ __ __ __

it will be set free from its __ __ __ __ __ __ __

Look up and read Genesis 3:17. What do you learn was cursed when Adam and Eve sinned?

the __ __ __ __ __ __

Read Romans 8:22. How does the creation respond to its slavery and corruption?

it __ __ __ __ __ __ and __ __ __ __ __ __ __

THINK ABOUT IT...

When God created the heavens and the earth they were good. When Adam and Eve disobeyed God sin did not just enter them, it entered the whole world. The serpent, Eve, the ground, and Adam were all cursed because of sin. The earth was created to glorify God and to provide the needs of mankind. After sin came, the earth began to die. Today we have tornadoes, hurricanes, earthquakes, droughts, and fires. Today trees die, flowers die, and crops die. Today animals attack, bugs bite, and fish eat each other. This is not the way God created it to be. So even the earth groans and suffers and longs to be free from death and be made new.

Read Romans 8:23. Who else groans?

_ _ _   _ _ _ _ _ _ _ _ _ _ groan within

_ _ _ _ _ _ _ _ _ _ _, waiting eagerly

What are we waiting eagerly for?

the _ _ _ _ _ _ _ _ _ _ of our _ _ _ _

Read Romans 8:24-25. How do we wait?

with _ _ _ _

Read Romans 8:26. Who helps us while we wait?

the _ _ _ _ _ _

Read Romans 8:26-27. Let's pay close attention to what we learn about the Spirit of God in this passage. How does He help us and why does He help us? There is chart below. Finish filling in the "How" and the "Why"

HOW	WHY
helps our _ _ _ _ _ _ _ _ _	we are not yet in our new bodies (Romans 8:23)
_ _ _ _ _ _ _ _ _ _ _ for us	we do not know how to _ _ _ _ as we should
searches _ _ _ _ _ and intercedes for the _ _ _ _ _ _	He knows what the _ _ _ _ _ of God is

THINK ABOUT IT...

How awesome is it that when we belong to Jesus, the Holy Spirit comes and lives inside of us and helps us. He helps us pray and He helps us hope. He helps us while we wait to get our new bodies to go with our new heart. Jesus promised us that He would send us a Helper and He always keeps His promises.

*Take a moment to look up and read **John 14:16-17**. Then take a moment to tell Jesus thank you for keeping His promise.*

****

DIGGING INTO ROMANS 8:28-30

28 And we know that God causes all things to work together for good to those who love God, to those who are called according to *His* purpose.

29 For those whom He foreknew, He also predestined *to become* conformed to the image of His Son, so that He would be the firstborn among many brethren;

30 and these whom He predestined, He also called; and these whom He called, He also justified; and these whom He justified, He also glorified

Have you ever wondered why bad things happen? We may not always know why some things happen, but as we look at our verse today we will learn something that will help.

Read Romans 8:28. What does this verse tell us that we should know?

we know that God causes __ __ __ __ __ __ __ __ __ to work together for __ __ __ __

Did this verse say that all things were good? Circle your answer.

Yes   No

Who does this verse say that God will cause all things to work together for good for?

those who __ __ __ __ God

those who are __ __ __ __ __ according to His __ __ __ __ __ __ __

According to Romans 8:28 what can we know that God will do with all the things that happen to those who love Him? Use the space below to answer in your own words or draw a picture to answer.

Read Romans 8:29. Why would God choose to cause all things to work together for good? Whose image is He making us into?

the image of His __ __ __

THINK ABOUT IT...

Have you ever played with play-do? If you have any at home go get some and come right back. Have you got it?

Do you have a mold for the play-do or maybe a cookie cutter? If you do, go get it, and come right back. Have you got it?

Okay, now look at the play-doh; squish it in your hands. Right now, that play do is like you before you have Jesus. It's formless and without a purpose.

Now look at your mold or cookie cutter. That mold is an image of something right?

When you take the play-do and try to put it into that mold you have to tear away the parts of the play-do that do not fit. As you fit the play-do into the mold, you are conforming it into the image.

This is kind of like how God conforms us into the image of His Son. Sometimes He has to tear things away from us, some times He has to squish and shove us, some times He has to press us... but it all will work together for good and eventually we will look like the image of His Son.

*Once you get all the play-do in the mold or cookie cutter set it down and read **Romans 8:30.***

Read Romans 8:30 and complete the list below.

those whom He predestined He also __ __ __ __ __ __

those He called He also __ __ __ __ __ __ __ __ __

those He justified He also __ __ __ __ __ __ __ __ __

Look at your play-do again. Take a moment to slowly pull the mold or cookie cutter away from the play-do. When the mold is removed does the play-do now keep the image? The play-do no longer is formless and without purpose. It now looks like something! It looks like the image it was conformed into. When we are finally glorified, when we finally get our new bodies, we will finally look like Jesus.

Look up and read 1 John 3:2-3. When Jesus appears who will we be like?

We will be like __ __ __

According to this verse, if we believe this, really believe this, then how should it affect our life?

everyone who has this hope fixed on Him __ __ __ __ __ __ __ __ himself

How can we purify our self? Look up and read 1John 1:9 to find out. Is there anything you need to talk to God about it? If there is, do it now.

****

DIGGING INTO ROMANS 8:31-39

31 What then shall we say to these things? If God *is* for us, who *is* against us?

32 He who did not spare His own Son, but delivered Him over for us all, how will He not also with Him freely give us all things?

33 Who will bring a charge against God's elect? God is the one who justifies;

34 who is the one who condemns? Christ Jesus is He who died, yes, rather who was raised, who is at the right hand of God, who also intercedes for us.

35 Who will separate us from the love of Christ? Will tribulation, or distress, or persecution, or famine, or nakedness, or peril, or sword?

36 Just as it is written, "For Your sake we are being put to death all day long; We were considered as sheep to be slaughtered."

37 But in all these things we overwhelmingly conquer through Him who loved us.

38 For I am convinced that neither death, nor life, nor angels, nor principalities, nor things present, nor things to come, nor powers,

39 nor height, nor depth, nor any other created thing, will be able to separate us from the love of God, which is in Christ Jesus our Lord.

It's almost time to finish Part Three of our study. These last verses are some of my favorite in the whole Bible.

DISCOVERING WHAT IT MEANS TO BE SAVED

Read Romans 8:31-34. How many questions are asked in these verses? Circle your answer.

1   3   4   5   7

Now let's look at them one by one.

1) What shall we say to these things?

What things? Could it be all the things that we have learned in Romans from chapter 1 all the way up to chapter 8? Circle your answer.

Yes   No

2) If God *is* for us, who *is* against us?

If God is for you, can anyone come against you? Circle your answer.

Yes   No

3) He who did not spare His own Son, but delivered Him over for us all, how will He not also with Him freely give us all things?

If God loved us so much that He gave His Son for us, do you think that He will also help us in every thing else in our lives? Circle your answer.

Yes   No

4) Who will bring a charge against God's elect?

If God has said you are forgiven? If God has said you are free? Is there anyone who can change that? Circle your answer.

Yes   No

5) God is the one who justifies; who is the one who condemns?

If God has said you are saved, can anyone else say you are not? Circle your answer.

Yes   No

Read Romans 8:34 again. In Romans 8:26-27 we learned that the Holy Spirit intercedes for us. Who we do learn also intercedes for us in Romans 8:34?

— — — — — —   — — — — — —

Read Romans 8:35-36. This verse asks the question, who will separate us from the love of Christ? Read through these verses and list the things that it says <u>WILL NOT</u> separate us from the love of Christ.

_____

_____

_____

_____

_____

_____

_____

Read Romans 8:37. According to this verse how do we respond to all these things listed in Romans 8:35-36?

we overwhelmingly __ __ __ __ __ __ __ through __ __ __ who __ __ __ __ __ us.

Read Romans 8:38-39. What else are we to be convinced of that can <u>never separate us</u> from the love of God?

neither __ __ __ __ __

nor __ __ __ __

nor __ __ __ __ __ __

nor __ __ __ __ __ __ __ __ __ __ __ __ __

nor things __ __ __ __ __ __ __

nor things to __ __ __ __

nor __ __ __ __ __ __

nor __ __ __ __ __ __

nor __ __ __ __ __

nor any other __ __ __ __ __ __ __   __ __ __ __ __

THINK ABOUT IT...

*Wow! Is there anything left that could separate us from the love of God in Christ Jesus? So if nothing can separate us, can we ever lose our salvation? Will Jesus ever leave us? Look up and read **Hebrews 13:5**. I think it's time for a big "Thank You" to our God! Let's close our study of Romans 6-8 by singing God a song right now. How about "Jesus loves me, this I know, for the Bible tells me so!"*

ABOUT THE AUTHOR

Nicole Love Halbrooks Vaughn is the founder of Proven Path Ministries. She has been married to Patrick Vaughn for seventeen years. They have three beautiful girls together. Nicole is a trained Precept Ministries Bible Study Leader. She has been leading Precept studies since 2004. She is a speaker and writer and faithfully serves with her family at their home church, Central Baptist, in Decatur, AL.